THE RELEVANCE OF CREATION

A Self-Instruction Program

(Includes Transparency Masters, General Instructions and Audio Cassette)

Master Books

Relevance Of Creation: Self-Instruction Program

Published by

Master Books
A Division of Creation Life Publishers, Inc.
P.O. Box 1606
El Cajon, California 92022

ISBN 0-89051-141-1

General Instructions

The following is an edited version of the message contained on the tape included in this instructional program. Throughout the script the positions at which the numbered overhead transparency masters were used in the original lecture are clearly indicated.

Because the "Relevance of Creation" message is such a vital one for Christians, this program has been published so others can give this message in their church, Bible study group, youth group, etc. Or, one can simply hand the taped message and the accompanying book of transparency masters to others so that they can benefit from the full thrust of this important presentation of the Gospel.

It is highly recommended that the book "The Lie: Evolution" by Ken Ham (published by Master Books, P.O. Box 1606, El Cajon, CA 92022) be carefully read before giving this presentation. Most of the transparency masters are from diagrams in this book which covers the "Relevance of Creation" message in detail, but also at a level easily understood.

Mr. Ham has given lectures on this topic for many years, and is very successfully awakening Christians to the importance of the creation/evolution issue in the Gospel presentation. It is only after hearing the "relevance" message that many Christians and non-Christians will look further at Genesis and Biblical authority. Thus, the message is the stimulant to introduce a complete program on who the Creator is and our relationship to Him.

This relevance of Creation message (with animated version of these diagrams) is also available in the 16mm Film, The Genesis Solution. (Films for Christ, 2628 W. Birchwood Circle, Mesa, AZ 85202, 1-800-332-2261)

To make overhead transparencies, simply use the special photocopier transparencies readily available for most modern photocopiers. To enhance the transparencies, colored overhead projector pens can be used to highlight various parts of each overhead.

THE RELEVANCE OF CREATION

(Start tape and follow the lecture using this edited transcript. It is suggested that you stop the tape when each new diagram is introduced so you can familiarize yourself with the concept(s) represented.)

I want to explain to you why I see the creation/evolution issue as important. Does it really matter what you believe about creation and evolution? Does it really matter what you believe about Genesis?

TRANSPARENCY #1

I find that many church-goers say creation/evolution is just an interesting side issue, and that there are more important issues in society; for example, homosexuality, pornography, abortion, and lawlessness. Many say that the gospel needs to be presented to this pagan world, so why bother about creation/evolution anyway?

Most people do not understand a lot of scientific terminology and thus think the issues of origins is beyond them. They believe this topic is just for the scientist and not for the average Christian.

TRANSPARENCY #2

One of the things that we need to get across to such people is that what is happening at the level of creation/evolution is foundational to all of those issues listed above. To understand what is happening in relation to the increase in lawlessness, homosexuality, pornography and abortion, one needs to understand what is happening at the level of origins (creation/evolution).

How does one connect creation/evolution to these particular issues? To start with, it must be understood that evolution is really not science. In fact, it is plain straight religion. The average Christian doesn't seem to understand that. Ask the average person the question—"What is science?" and try to get them to write down a definition! Most couldn't do this. If you don't know what science is and what it isn't, then how do you know whether scientists are being scientific in what they say? For example, a scientist can make certain claims about the age of the earth, or the age of fossils. If a person doesn't know what science is and how to apply science's limitations, how will they discern whether what is being stated is real science — or whether it is conjecture based on various assumptions?

We often hear of the situation where evolutionists state that creation can't be truth in science classes because it is religion, whereas evolution is true science.

TRANSPARENCY #3

However, evolution is also a religion. This reality is something that we need to come to grips with. A reasonable definition of science is:

> Science is the total collection of knowledge gained by man's observations of the physical world, using one or more of his five senses, taste, smell, sight, hearing, or touch, to investigate the world that only exists in the present, and observations can be repeated. Thus a scientist uses his five senses to investigate the world and find out information about the world.

From my experience the average high school student cannot give a concise definition of science. I have found that their definitions range all the way from "hacking up cats, cutting up frogs, and looking down microscopes," to "boring."

TRANSPARENCY #4

All fossils EXIST in the present. When scientists dig up fossils, they are not digging up the PAST but the PRESENT. When you observe fossils (whether in a museum or in the field in rock strata), you are observing evidence that exists in the present. The pictures the scientists draw to explain the fossils (e.g.: drawings of swamps with the various animals and plants existing in a supposedly ancient environment millions of years ago) is only a story (conjecture). They did not see the organisms living. Nor was there anyone there millions of years ago to take pictures and record observations. When a scientist digs up fossils, they are dead; they don't have pictures or labels with them. When it comes to the past then, we need to realize that we do not have the past. We only have the present. According to the theory of evolution, no observer was there millions of years ago to see the supposed events of evolution occurring. No witness was there to record the events to hand down to scientists. No animals turn into people. Real science involves what you can repeatably test in the present.

Evolution can be defined as a belief about the past based on the words of scientists who don't know everything, who were not there, and who are trying to explain how the evidence, which only exists in the present, got there. When some famous scientist says that they know what happened millions of years ago and that creationists are wrong, remember, they were NOT there! They can't scientifically prove what allegedly happened millions of years ago.

How can anyone ever have the ability of coming to the right conclusion about anything—past, present, or future? The only way to be 100 per cent right about anything—would be if you knew everything, that is, if you were omniscient. It is easy to come to wrong conclusions when watching a murder mystery on TV, for instance, simply because you don't have all the evidence. That is why the outcome can often be a surprise—something you did not think of or think possible because you did not know everything. Thus, if you don't have all the evidence you can end up with the wrong conclusion.

Herein lies a problem all humans have. No matter how much we know, there could be an infinite amount more to know. The point is, we don't know how much more there is to know—which means we don't know how much we do or don't know in relation to how much there is to know. This basically means humans don't know much at all. Thus, if we do not have all of the evidence, how do we know for sure we can come to right conclusions about things—particularly concerning things that supposedly happened in the past with no infallible human observer present?

How, therefore, can a scientist know truth? This dilemma can only be solved if one has access to all knowledge. Regardless of what others say, the Bible claims to be the Word of such a One. This book claims to be the Word of God who knows everything. The words of this book say that God (an infinite being—infinite in wisdom and knowledge) moved people by His Spirit to write the words in this book. We are told that God does not tell a lie and that He is omniscient (all knowing). If this claim is true, it means that the only way one could ever be sure of coming to the right conclusion about anything is by starting with the information revealed in this book and building a whole philosophy (your whole way of thinking—a complete framework of understanding) on what the Bible says and not on what fallible humans say.

TRANSPARENCY #6

One of the problems that exists in many churches today, is that instead of starting with the Word of One who knows everything, and building understanding on that, many Christians start with human opinions. The church needs to abandon this opinion-oriented philosophy that pervades society and recognize that the ONLY way you could ever come to a right conclusion about anything, is by starting with the Word of One who knows everything. **If you don't have an absolute, you really don't have anything. You can never know for sure about anything.**

Christians must also realize that all humans are sinful beings who do not know everything. Only God does. Therefore, to come to right conclusions about this world, to understand geology, geography, fossils, morality, in fact anything, we must start with what God's Word says.

TRANSPARENCY #7

The very first book in the Bible, **Genesis,** is an account of the origins and history of all life and the universe. It tells of the creation of different kinds of animals and plants and of the creation of Adam and Eve, the first people. This book explains the entrance of sin and death into the world, and a judgment by water when a world-wide flood destroyed the original world. We are told of the event of the "Tower of Babel" that is important in understanding cultures and nations existing today. **Knowing** what happened in the past can give us a basis for explaining the present. If we start with what has been **revealed** about the events of the past, one has the ability to come to some right conclusions about geology, cultures, geography, biology, etc. **If we have the revealed Word of One who knows everything, then a basis exists for having right interpretations about the facts of the present.**

If anyone ignores the revealed Word of One with infinite knowledge, then he has no basis for determining truth – he can never know for sure whether his interpretations are right.

Genesis is foundational in understanding science and history. However, the book of Genesis is one of the most disbelieved and attacked books in both Christian and non-Christian circles. Yet, Genesis is also the most quoted-from or referred to book in the entire Bible. Consider John 5:45-47, where Jesus Christ said "Do not think that I will accuse you to the Father: there is one that accuseth you, even Moses, in whom ye trust. For had ye believed Moses, ye would have believed me: for he wrote of me. But if ye believe not his writings, how shall ye believe my words?" In Luke 16:31 Jesus quotes Abraham as saying, "If they hear not Moses and the prophets, neither will they be persuaded, though one rose from the dead". In Luke 24:27 we read "And beginning at

Moses and all the prophets, He (Jesus) expounded unto them in all the Scriptures the things concerning Himself." At the end of Acts, we read where Paul preached about Jesus Christ from Moses and the prophets. Why is it then that one book of the writings of Moses, Genesis, is the most quoted from yet the most attacked?

The psalmist in Psalm 11:3 states, "If the foundations are destroyed, what can the righteous do?"

TRANSPARENCIES #8 AND 9

Consider the foundation of a structure such as a house. If the foundation is destroyed (e.g.: by an earthquake), then the structure will no longer stand. Think about the nation you live in. From a Christian perspective, the moral fabric (Christian structure) is collapsing. The family unit is also collapsing. The two are very much related because the family is really the backbone of a nation. The structures are collapsing because the foundations are being eroded and destroyed. We need to look in detail at what these foundations consist of and what is happening.

TRANSPARENCY #10

Many church-going people appear to be ignorant of the fact that all Christian doctrine, (what Christians believe) is founded in the book of Genesis. Every single Biblical doctrine of theology, directly or indirectly, has its foundation in the book of Genesis.

TRANSPARENCIES #10 AND 11

The meaning of anything is tied up in its origin. The meaning of marriage is tied up with its origin in Genesis. This is also true of death, sin, the seven day week, why Jesus died on a cross, clothes, dominion — all doctrines ultimately have their foundation in the book of Genesis.

TRANSPARENCY #12

Logically then, the Christian framework (like its doctrines) can stand only when the foundation exists. But, if the foundation was removed, then the Christian structure would ultimately collapse.

Christian parents want the Christian structure to be built in the next generation (their children). However, if they try to build this framework in their children without a foundation—it will not easily stand. There are whole generations of Christian families where the children are rebelling against Christianity—the structure is collapsing.

You can't build a house from the roof down, yet many Christians build the structure in the next generation from the roof down, instead of the foundation up!

TRANSPARENCY #13

Sadly, when these children then go to a public educational institution and are taught the foundation of evolution (which, as we will see, will not allow the Christian structure to stand), many reject Christianity and the structure collapses. Many parents have noticed that the decline in their children's interest in Christianity went hand in hand with increasing levels of education in public schools, colleges, etc. What is the bottom-line issue when it comes to the different foundations of creation and evolution?

TRANSPARENCY #14

1. **Creation**: The fact that there is a Creator means that He owns everything—He owns each person. He has total right over our lives and has a right to set the rules (and thus tell us what is right and wrong) because He is the Creator—the Absolute Authority. We can know what is good and bad, because there is ONE who is good and who can therefore define right and wrong. All humans need to submit themselves totally to the One Who owns them. Nothing is a matter of just mere human opinion.

TRANSPARENCY # 15

2. **Evolution**: In most instances through the media and public education system this is taught as an atheistic theory to explain the origin of life. This anti-God religion teaches that humans are products of properties inherent in matter and the chance processes of millions of years. Logically then, there is no absolute authority—no one owns you. People can write their own rules and have their own opinions about anything. There is no absolute authority who has a right to impose rules on anyone. Therefore, the more people who believe there is no God who owns them, the more they will become consistent in their thinking and be like the Israelites described in the book of Judges. There we are told that when they had no King to tell them what to do, they all did what was right in their own eyes.

To a vast majority of people in our society, the King has been dethroned. The accepted norm is that everyone should tolerate everyone else's opinions. This also means that they must be intolerant of any Christian who says that God sets the rules and all must obey Him. Society has a new god (human wisdom), and the doctors of science who promote atheistic evolution — an anti-God religion, the implications of which are that people believe they are answerable to no one but themselves. The result of this teaching is that people will begin to question the Christian ethics in relation to the purposes and meaning of life. They insist that they can do or be whatever they determine. Doing what is right in their own eyes, abort babies, be a homosexual, take drugs, etc.

We need to realize the seriousness of this situation. When educators claim they have thrown religion out of the science classroom by eliminating creation, in reality they have thrown Christianity out and replaced it with a new religion — humanism! This is the philosophy that is pervading the nations of the world. Unfortunately the church by and large is doing little about this situation because most Christians, including most pastors, do not understand what is happening at the foundational level. They do not recognize that evolution is an anti-Christian, anti-God religion, and they have been led to believe by the educational system and media propaganda that it is real science. They think Genesis can't be trusted.

To illustrate the importance of Genesis as discussed above, let us look more in detail at two specific examples.

TRANSPARENCY #16 AND #10 COMBINED

Marriage: In Matthew 19 we read that Jesus was asked a question concerning divorce. He answered the question in verses 4 and 5, "Have ye not read, that he which made them at the beginning made them male and female, And said, for this cause shall a man leave father and mother, and shall cleave to his wife: and they twain shall be one flesh?" Jesus quoted from Genesis to give the foundation (thus the reason) for marriage. Starting with the origin of marriage in Genesis we learn a number of aspects concerning this doctrine:

a. **The spiritual meaning of the marriage tie** — God took dust and made man. He took part of the man's side and made a woman. A husband and wife are **one** in marriage, but man and woman were one flesh historically. If it wasn't so historically, then the spiritual meaning of oneness is not valid. A man and a woman are to cleave unto each other as if they had no parents, just like Adam and Eve who had no parents.

b. **The origin of the family unit** — a male and a female, one man for one woman for life. Why must marriage be between a male and a female and not a male and a male, or two females? God made man and woman and thus sets the rules. God made marriage and gave the man and woman their roles. God made Adam and Eve — a man and a woman as the basis of the family. He did not make two men or two women as the basis of the family. That is why Paul teaches in Romans 1 that homosexuality is perverse and anti-God; it destroys the family.

c. **The importance of marriage** — One of the primary concerns of marriage is found in Malachi 2:15. In the context of this passage we understand that the Israelites had taken pagan wives, and brought idols into their homes. They were destroying the meaning of the family unit as God had ordained it. Through the prophet God asked them why He made the two one originally (a reference to the creation of man and woman in Genesis). He then answered by saying that the reason for this was because He sought godly offspring from their union. These godly offspring are meant to influence the world for Jesus Christ and produce similar godly offspring themselves. This should be the case generation after generation. However, in many Christian homes we do not see **Godly** offspring.

d. **Roles** — one of the major reasons there is such a tremendous breakdown in the Christian family today is because the roles God made for husband and wife (father and mother) in Genesis are not adhered to. It must be understood that concerning the roles of mother and father, God sets the rules because He is the Creator and made marriage. Many husbands and wives have their own opinions concerning their roles rather than obeying the rules God gave for their role in marriage. For marriages to work, both the husband and the wife must be prepared to accept the roles ordained by God, rather than their own opinions.

(1) **Woman's role.** The Bible explicitly states that Adam was created first, and Eve was deceived, therefore a woman is to be in submission to her husband. Many women do not want to be in submission to their husbands. However, it is not a matter of one's opinion, but a matter of obeying the rules God gave for marriage. For the marriage to work, and children to see the example of the correct roles (so they will learn these roles) the Bible must be obeyed. Some think this means that a man is superior to the woman. The Bible teaches that men and women are **equal** in God's sight, yet it is not a matter of equality, but of **roles.**

(2) **Man's role.** The husband is told to love his wife as Christ loved the church and gave Himself for it. Husbands need to exhibit this to their wife and so their children can see it. There is a very special role for husband and father which is NOT being obeyed in many homes to-day. In Isaiah 38:19 we read that "the fathers to the children shall make known thy truth". Ephesians 6:4 states, "Fathers bring your children up in the nurture and admonition of the Lord." It

is obvious from many passages of Scripture (both Old and New Testament) that fathers are to be the spiritual head of the house, instructing their children, and being a priest to their wives and families.

However, if one asks who, in the majority of Christian homes, leads the spiritual upbringing of the children, the answer without fail is "the mother." This means there is something drastically wrong with the men of today's Christian families. And what is the end result of fathers not taking their God-given responsibility of headship? The structure in the next generation will collapse! Psalm 78 emphasizes the importance of fathers passing information on to the next generation, so they will pass it on to the next and so on. Fathers are held responsible for transmitting knowledge to the next generation, so it can be transmitted generation after generation.

What can happen as a result of fathers failing to pass on the right training and knowledge can be seen reflected in the Australian Aborigines. When they were first discovered they were an anti-God spiritist culture. And yet, their distant ancestor was Noah and, farther back, Adam. Noah had the knowledge of God, knew how to build ships, etc. What happened in history to produce a culture that worshipped evil spirits and had degenerated to only using stone tools? Somewhere in their history, knowledge of God and technology was not transmitted to the next generation. Thus the culture became a spiritually degenerate culture perpetuating this generation after generation. If you think about it, it only takes one generation to produce a so-called primitive or spiritually degenerate culture. It only takes one generation of fathers not transmitting knowledge to their children and the culture degenerates spiritually. It would only take one generation going through the modern public education system, devoid of any mention of God, to produce a spiritually degenerate culture in today's world.

Christian fathers need to obey the Scriptures and train their children the way the Bible commands—but very few fathers probably even know what the Bible instructs on this matter. Many think the psychologists know best about how to train children. However, if what the psychologists say disagrees with the Bible, then the psychologists are wrong! God is the Creator and He sets the rules.

The Christian church needs to wake up and understand that in every area of life, our thinking should be built on the foundation of God's Word, not human opinion—whether the matter is abortion, women's role in the church, the election of deacons, how to run a business, or whatever.

TRANSPARENCIES #17 AND #10 COMBINED

Why do people wear clothes? If it is because of opinions such as "it's cold" or "it's hot", then standards would be whatever a person made them. No one should be made to wear clothes if they don't want to, if this issue is based on human opinion.

However, we actually wear clothes because God gave clothes. The origin of clothing is found in the book of Genesis. Because of Adam's action in eating the forbidden fruit, sin entered the world. Sin distorts everything — including nakedness. As a result of sin, God gave Adam and Eve coats — the first blood sacrifice as a covering for their sin (a picture of what was to come in the sacrifical death of the Lord Jesus Christ). If God gave clothes because of sin, then it follows there must be standards for the origin of clothing. In the New Testament this is made clear where we are told that if a man lusts after a woman in his heart, he commits adultery. The reason men are singled out is because they respond sexually very easily to a woman's body. This is the way men were made. However, because of sin, this created feature is distorted and men do have a problem called lust. Job recognized this, for in Job 31:1 Job says that he has a covenant with his eyes so he will not lust upon a maiden.

The point is that men and women were created differently, and the man does respond to a woman's body very easily. Originally this was to be in a perfect relationship with one woman, his wife. Now sin distorts that, and it is important to realize that what a female wears or doesn't wear can put a stumbling block in a man's way and cause him to commit adultery in his heart.

Fathers need to explain to their daughters what men are like — otherwise they may respond only to fashions of the day or peer pressure. Sadly, in many Christian homes the battle between parents and daughters over standards of clothing is often just a battle between opposing opinions. Parents need to teach from a foundational perspective of Genesis so their children will have the necessary basis for Godly decisions.

I have had many parents say that their children have rebelled against Christianity saying, "Why should we obey your rules?" The parents, after hearing a message on the relevance of creation, then realized that they had never taught their children that the rules were not theirs, but God's. Because this foundational teaching was missing, the Christian structure did not stand in the next generation.

TRANSPARENCY #18

To sum up so far then — if Adam was our ancestor, then it means God sets the rules because He is the Creator. If, on the other hand, man's ancestor was an ape and there is no God, then everyone has a right to their own opinion and can set their own rules. Many nations of the world were once built on the foundation that God is Creator and thus His rules should be the one to govern society.

TRANSPARENCY #19

If God is Creator, then:

1. There are definite laws to abide by;
2. The roles for men in marriage have been set by God — marriage has a basis and therefore meaning;
3. Clothing was given because of sin and therefore there are dress standards consistent with the moral basis of clothing;
4. Life has meaning and purpose because their God is the Creator.

If life is the result of chance random processes (atheistic evolution) then:

1. Laws are only opinions — thus the laws that stand will depend on who can enforce their opinions;
2. Marriage is only an opinion so homosexuality is an acceptable alternative;
3. Wearing clothing is dependent upon one's opinion, so standards are whatever a person makes them — one doesn't have to wear clothes if one can get away with it;
4. Life has no meaning and thus no purpose; therefore, abortion should be allowed if humans are only animals and each person owns his/her own body — there is no God who is Creator and who owns anyone.

TRANSPARENCY #20

Thus the more the foundation of God as Creator is removed from society and replaced with the religion of evolution, it would be expected that more people would reject the Christian absolutes (marriage, standards of clothing, purpose, etc.) and accept abortion, homosexuality, etc. This is exactly what is happening. People consider that their own opinions about anything should be accepted. It is important to realize, though, that I am not blaming evolution for abortion or homosexuality. It is the rejection of God as Creator and the rejection of His rules that logically lead to people accepting these anti-God philosophies.

This then helps us realize that in regard to the AIDS issue, it is really a morality problem and not just a disease problem. To solve the problem in regard to the spread of AIDS, people need to obey the laws that God gave in regard to sex and marriage.

TRANSPARENCY #21

Consider two castles. The first one has the foundation of evolution and the structure of humanism is built upon that with the issues of abortion, homosexuality, lawlessness, etc., emanating from that structure.

The second castle has the foundation of creation, and the structure of Christianity (all Christian doctrine) is built upon that.

What then is happening in society? The evolutionists are knocking out the foundation of creation, and the structure of Christianity is collapsing. The Christians are responding by shooting at each other, shooting off into nowhere, or shooting at the issues. Many Christians do try to fight abortion, etc., but at an issue level, not a foundational level. Even if Christians did get the laws changed in regard to the present legalization of abortion, when the next generation comes through who believe in evolution even more, they will just change the laws back again.

Too many Christians are taking pot-shots at the balloons, instead of attacking the foundation of humanism—evolution. To be successful in destroying the castle of humanism, the guns need to be aimed and fired at the foundation of evolution. At the same time, Christians need to be rebuilding the foundation of creation so the Christian structure can be rebuilt.

However, there are many Christians saying "Why can't we just believe that God used evolution?" This is a very common belief among the churches of today. The Bible, though, teaches quite clearly that death came into the world after Adam sinned, and not millions of years before man evolved (Romans 5:12-14).

TRANSPARENCY #22

In fact, the very reason for death is because God, as a God of love, provided a means for man's deliverance because of sin. When man (in Adam) rebelled against God (the entrance of sin), he died spiritually immediately. He was cut off from God, and would have remained so for eternity. In addition to death (separation), God provided a means by which man could come back to God to spend eternity with Him.

In Hebrews 9:22 we read that "Without the shedding of blood there can be no remission of sins." God introduced death and bloodshed so man could be redeemed. There was no death and bloodshed before Adam fell. In fact, if death and bloodshed had existed before Adam sinned, the message of redemption would be nonsense. God, in love, introduced death so we could die and leave our sinful bodies; so Jesus Christ could come and die and shed His precious blood on a cross and be raised from the dead; so we could spend eternity with Him.

TRANSPARENCY #23

The evolutionary process has death and struggle (bloodshed) over millions of years, eventually resulting in man coming into existence. The evolutionist sees today's world of death and suffering as an evolutionary one. The Bible teaches that the world we see is a **cursed** one. It is a world originally created in a perfect state by God and it has suffered the degenerative effects of the curse and the catastrophic effects of a global flood.

TRANSPARENCY #24

Thus, evolution and the Bible are in total conflict. The first would have us believe that death and bloodshed is the means by which man evolved. The Bible clearly teaches that death will be cancelled and man is redeemed! Therefore, evolution destroys and totally undermines the whole message of the Cross. Christians who believe in evolution need to recognize that they are really destroying the foundations of the Gospel message they are trying to preach.

Additional Resources

Once this message has been given, it is important to continue with follow up material. Here is a list of resources recommended to help you including books, tapes, videos and films. You are welcome to contact the **Institute for Creation Research** (10946 Woodside Ave. N., Santee, CA 92071, 619/448-0090) for more information.

The Lie: Evolution *by Ken Ham*
Change lives for Christ! Possibly the most powerful evangelistic book of the decade. Helps pastors, teachers, parents and students present the hope of the Gospel message to a generation blinded to the truth of God's Word.
Master Books/ Cloth/ 168 pages $12.95

Understanding Genesis — A Complete Creation Seminar
by Ken Ham and Gary Parker
Learn the historical and scientific accuracy of God's Word with this unique, professionally taped series. This powerful evangelistic and discipleship tool includes ten programs by two outstanding Creationist communicators bringing you dynamic instruction on foundational Christian issues. Guaranteed value for every Christian concerned about the truth of Genesis and its importance in our world today.
A seminar study guide is also available for $1.50.
CLP Video/ VHS only
TEN VIDEO CASSETTES — $250.00

Available 1989

A new book and Bible-study on the importance of Genesis

BACK TO GENESIS *by Ken Ham* (only $8.95)

Additional Resources

Creation Evangelism — An <u>Audio Learning Series Presentation</u> *by Ken Ham*
An important six-tape study covering the following: *Relevance of Creation, Creation: Facts and Bias - Parts 1 and 2, Six Days of Creation, Creation Evangelism, and Education-The Responsibility of Christians.*

Master Books/ Six Audio Tape Set $39.95

Relevance of Creation Video *by Ken Ham*
Part of the fifteen program <u>Creation Knowledge Video library</u>, this video presents Ken giving the relevance of the creation message.

CLP Video/ VHS only $19.95

CREATION KNOWLEDGE VIDEO LIBRARY — Additional Titles

Menace of Humanism *by Dr. Richard B. Bliss, Ed.D.*
What is True Science? *by Dr. Richard Bliss, Ed.D.*
Strange Case of the Woodpecker *by Gary Parker, Ed.D.*
Gish-Doolittle Debate *by Dr. Duane Gish, Ph.D.*
The Great Debate: Evolution or Creation *by A. E. Wilder-Smith*
Creation Programs for Children (5 selection/tape)
Creation Programs for Teens and Adults (4 programs)
More Creation Programs for Teen and Adults (4 programs)
Evolution: What do the Fossils Say? *by Luther Sunderland/John Read*
Evolution in Turmoil *by Henry M. Morris, Ph.D.*
Bible and Archaeology *by Clifford Wilson, Ph.D.*
Genesis Record *by Henry M. Morris, Ph.D.*
Science of Creation Part 1: Origin of the Universe *by Robert Gentry, Ph.D.*
Science of Creation Part 2: Origin of life *by Duane T. Gish, Ph.D.*
CLP Video/ VHS only $19.95

To place an order or receive your complete Creation Knowledge Catalog write or call:
Master Books ● CLP Video
P.O. Box 1606
El Cajon, CA 92022
619/448-1121

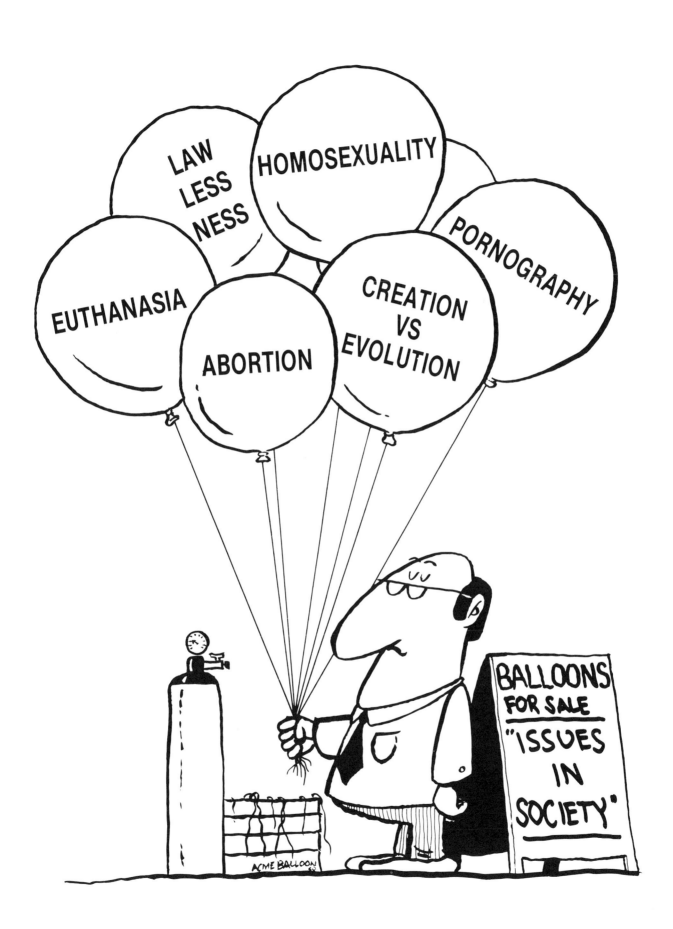

Transparency #1

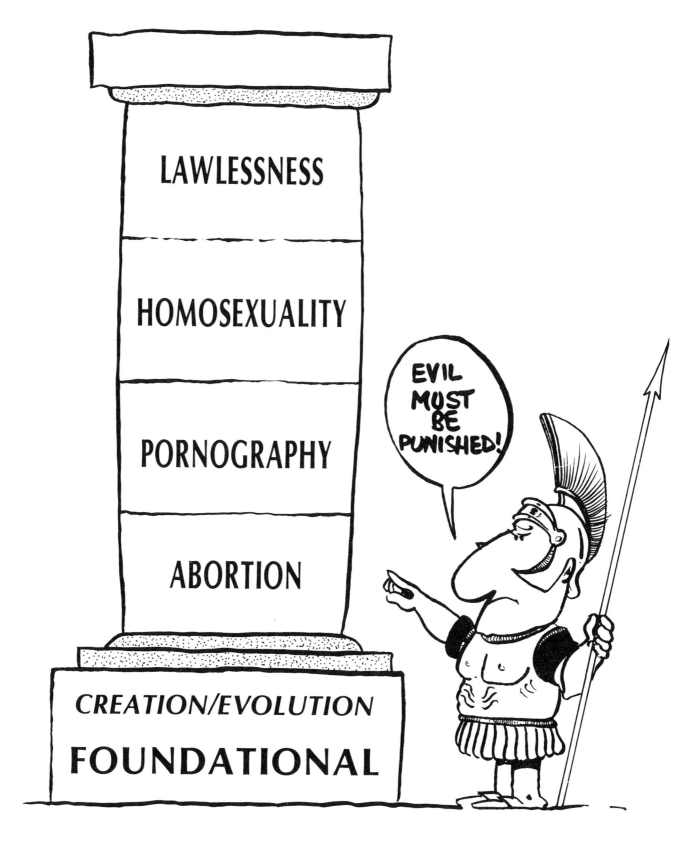

EVOLUTION
IS
RELIGION

IS EVOLUTION TRUE OR FALSE?

Transparency #5

Transparency #6

DAYS OF CREATION IN GENESIS ONE

DAY 1
(1 : 3-5)
LIGHT

DAY 2
(1 : 6-8)
WATER &
SKY

DAY 3
(1 : 9-13)
LAND &
VEGETATION

DAY 4
(1 : 14-19)
LUMINARIES
(sun, moon, stars)

DAY 5
(1 : 20-23)
FISH & BIRDS

DAY 6
(1 : 24-31)
BEASTS &
MAN

Transparency #8

Transparency #9

Transparency #10

DOCTRINE

NO FOUNDATIONS

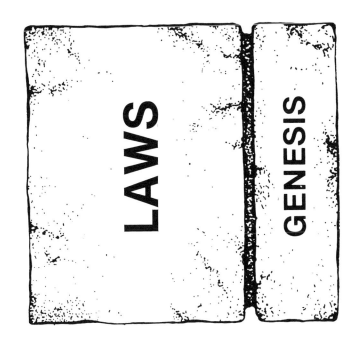

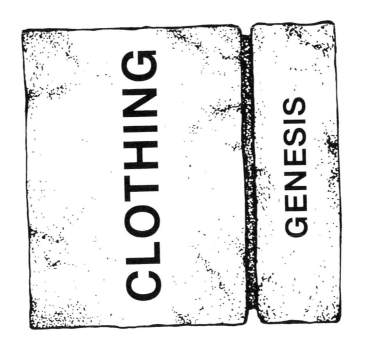

CLOTHING

GENESIS

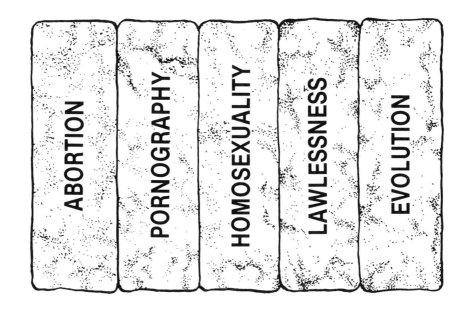

ABORTION PORNOGRAPHY HOMOSEXUALITY LAWLESSNESS EVOLUTION

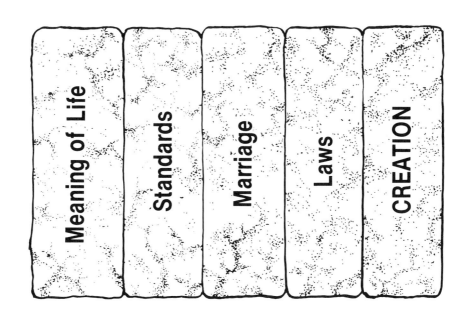

Meaning of Life Standards Marriage Laws CREATION

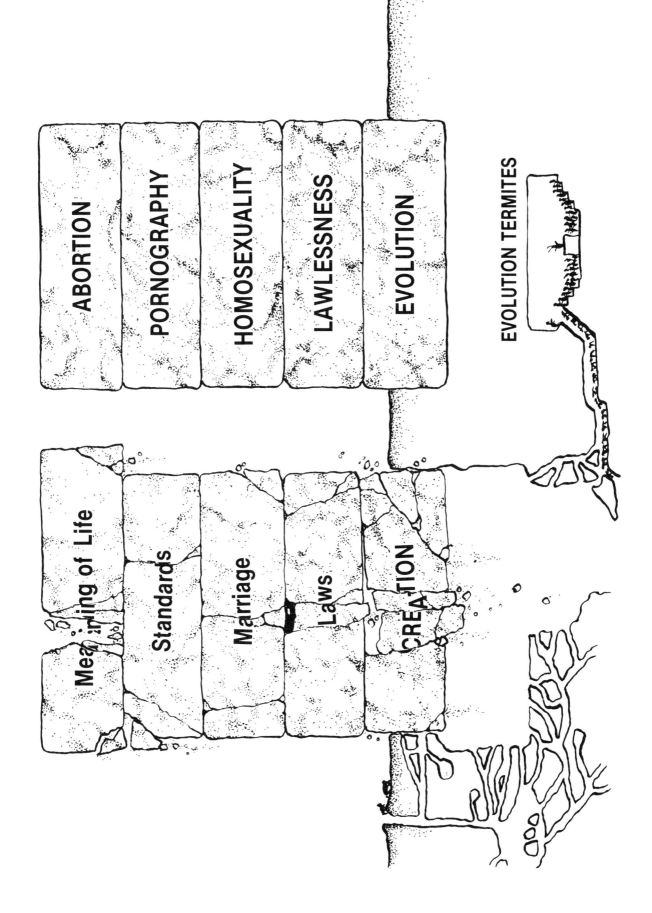

ABORTION

PORNOGRAPHY

HOMOSEXUALITY

LAWLESSNESS

EVOLUTION

EVOLUTION TERMITES

Meaning of Life

Standards

Marriage

Laws

CREATION

Transparency #20

Transparency #21

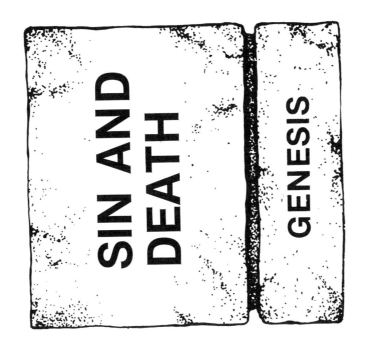

EVOLUTION

SCRIPTURE

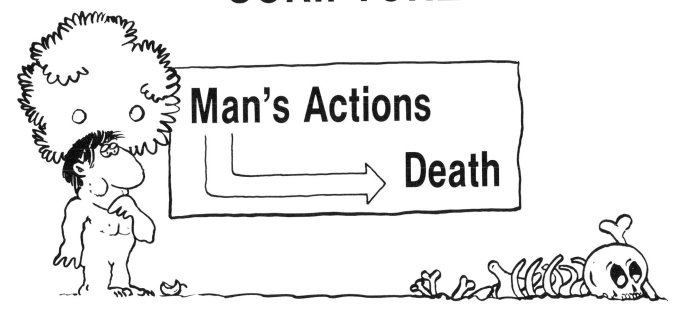

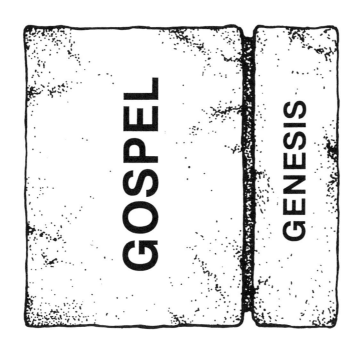

Additional
Transparency Masters

---
for teaching from

The Lie: Evolution

by Ken Ham

THE GOSPEL

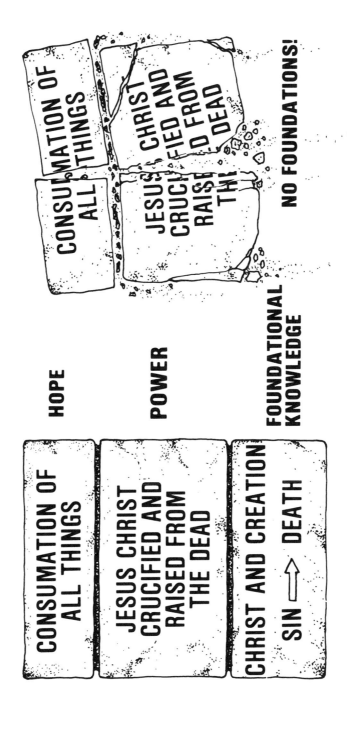

HOPE — CONSUMATION OF ALL THINGS

POWER — JESUS CHRIST CRUCIFIED AND RAISED FROM THE DEAD

FOUNDATIONAL KNOWLEDGE — CHRIST AND CREATION — SIN ⟹ DEATH

NO FOUNDATIONS!

	BASIS	INFLUENCE	BIAS
ATHEISM	NO GOD EXISTS	CAN'T CONSIDER CREATION	100%
AGNOSTIC	DON'T CARE CAN'T KNOW DON'T KNOW	MUST EXCLUDE DEFINITE ROLE OF GOD OPEN?	100%
THEISM	GOD DEDUCED	NO ABSOLUTES	100%
REVEALED	GOD REVEALED TO MAN	ABSOLUTE REFERENCE POINTS	100%

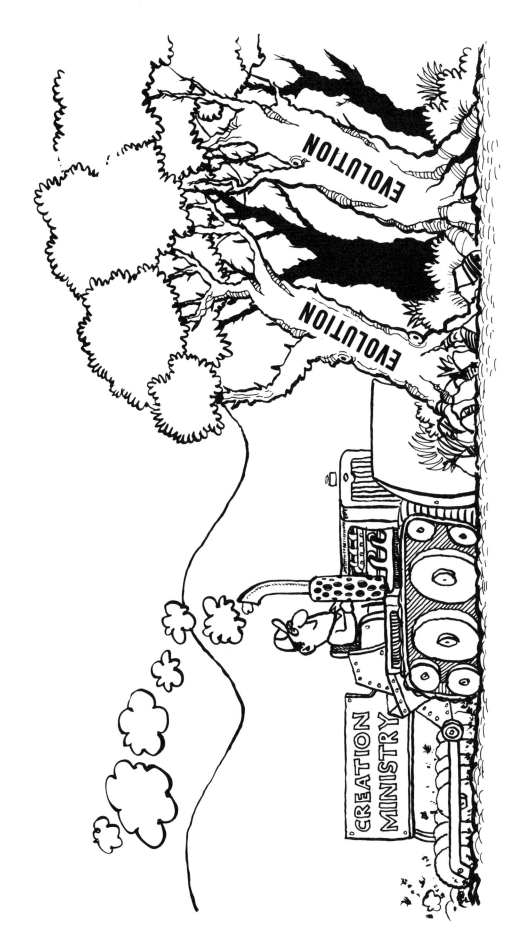

PAUL
ACTS:17

THE WORLD

CREATION

CRUCIFIXION AND RESURRECTION

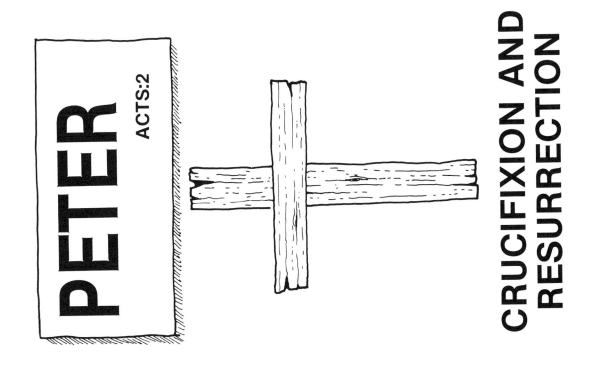

PETER
ACTS:2

CRUCIFIXION AND RESURRECTION